God's Little Book

Marriage
Builders

Karen & Bernie Holford

Dedicated to Beth and Tim Craggs

First published in 2010
Copyright © 2010 Autumn House
Publishing (Europe) Ltd
British Library Cataloguing in Publication Data.
A catalogue record for this book is available
from the British Library.
ISBN 978-1-906381-52-3
Published by Autumn House (Europe),
Grantham, Lincolnshire.
Designed by Abigail Murphy.
Printed in Thailand.
Bible verses have been taken from the *New International
Version* (Hodder and Stoughton) of the Bible.

The more you experience God's extravagant love for you, the more love you will have to share with your husband or wife.

This little book is an adventure into God's love and the difference he can make to your marriage.

'Dear friends, let us love
one another, for love
comes from God.'
1 John 4:7

God is the very creator of
love. He is the source of
every loving thing that
we do for one another.

Tell your spouse about a
time when you experienced
God's love for you and
describe how this inspired
your love for them.

Make an alphabetical list
of God's loving qualities.
Thank God for his incredible
love and the ways in which
it reverberates through
your marriage.

'The Lord God made a
woman from the rib he had
taken out of the man.'

Genesis 2:22

In order for God to create
a woman, a man had to
sacrifice a part of
his own body.

Think of your spouse as an important part of your own body. How does this idea change how you treat your husband or wife?

Do something to pamper your spouse's body. Offer a hand massage, bathe each other, or give each other a simple pedicure.

'This is now bone of my
bones and flesh of my flesh:
she shall be called
"woman".'

Genesis 2:23

When the man saw that
God had made woman out of
his own body, he gave her a
name that would always
remind them of their
physical bond.

What affectionate names do you use for one another? If you don't have any, what would you like to be called?

Talk about some of the affectionate names people have given you over the years and what those names mean to each of you now.

'For this reason a man will leave his father and mother and be united to his wife, and they will become one flesh.'

Genesis 2:24

Each of you needs to let go of any beliefs, expectations and behaviours from your own families that may hurt your marriage.

What beliefs, expectations
and behaviours from your
own family would your
spouse say you've brought
into your marriage?

Which of these bring you
closer to your husband
or wife, and which ones
are holding you back
from being as united
as you'd like to be?

'The **LORD** God said,
"It is not good for the
man to be alone." '
Genesis 2:18

Even in a perfect world,
where he spoke face to
face with God, Adam felt
lonely and in need of the
friendship of another
human being.

What can you do with your husband or wife so that they're less likely to feel lonely today?

Spend an hour together doing an activity that your spouse enjoys . . . even if it's not *your* favourite!

'The **LORD** God said,
"It is not good for the man
to be alone. I will make a
helper suitable for him." '

Genesis 2:18

The word that's been
translated in our Bibles
as 'helper' means someone
who comes alongside and
supports another person
as his or her equal.

What support does your
husband or wife most need
from you today?

Think of a task that your
spouse hates doing, and
then do it secretly, as a
surprise. Offer to help your
spouse with the job the
next time it needs doing.

'Where you go I will go,
and where you stay I
will stay. Your people
will be my people and
your God my God.'
Ruth 1:16

Making a commitment
means giving up our own
plans and doing what's best
for the one we love.

Discuss the dreams you share for the places where you'd like to live, work and worship in the future.

Which parts of your dreams could you incorporate into your lives this week, this month or this year?

'Each one should use
whatever gift he has
received to serve others.'
1 Peter 4:10

God has given each of
you unique gifts to bless
your marriage and
those around you.

**What spiritual gifts
has God given you
and your spouse?**

**How can you use these to
strengthen your marriage?
Discover a ministry
where you can serve
others together in a
way that makes the best
use of your unique gifts,
skills and passions.**

'Love is patient.'
1 Corinthians 13:4

**Love slows its own
step to match the other
person's pace.**

When do you most need
to be patient with your
spouse? What difference
would it make to your
marriage if you were
more patient?

Try going at your spouse's
slower pace and give them
the gift of working at a
speed that's more
comfortable for them.

'Love is kind.'

1 Corinthians 13:4

Love thinks of thoughtful
things to do for the
other person . . . and
then does them quietly,
without being asked.

What could you do to show
some thoughtful kindness
towards your spouse?

Take a few moments to
describe one of the kindest
things your husband or wife
has ever done for you.

'Love . . . is not rude.'
1 Corinthians 13:5

Love speaks words that
bless, not words that
insult or ridicule.

What words could you say
that would bless your
husband or wife?

Say something nice to your
spouse as often as you can.
Letters, cards, texts and
emails are other ways to
express your affection.

'Love . . . keeps no
record of wrongs.'
1 Corinthians 13:5

Love has a huge 'delete'
button for the other
person's mistakes.

Make a list of the things
your spouse does well.

Focusing your mind on the
items on this list will help
you to 'delete' from your
thought patterns some of
the mistakes they've
made in the past.

'Love . . . always protects.'
1 Corinthians 13:7

**Love creates a protective
shell around the other
person's vulnerability.**

When does your husband
or wife feel most in need
of your protection?
When does he or she feel
most vulnerable with
others, or even with you?

What can you do to
help the one you love
feel really safe?

'Love . . . always hopes.'
1 Corinthians 13:7

**Love always hopes . . . that
things will only get better.**

What hopes do you and your spouse have for your relationship? How can you both feel more hopeful about your marriage?

Write a list of the hopes you have for your marriage and the things you can do to help those hopes become a reality.

'Love . . . always
perseveres.'
1 Corinthians 13:7

Love never gives up.

In which area of your
marriage do you most
need to persevere?

List the benefits for you,
your spouse, your marriage,
family, church, community
and workplace that can
result from being willing to
persevere together to
make your marriage
the best it can be.

'Everyone should be quick
to listen, slow to speak
and slow to become angry.'
James 1:19

Many problems in
relationships can be
solved when we take the
time to listen to each
other's concerns.

If you took the time to listen to your husband or wife, what do you think they'd like to tell you?

Spend five minutes listening to your loved one without interrupting. Find ways to let them know that you're really hearing what they're saying.

'Do not let any
unwholesome talk come out
of your mouths, but only
what is helpful for building
others up according to
their needs, that it may
benefit those who listen.'
Ephesians 4:29

Our words can gently shape
our spouses into the people
they want to become.

What are your husband or wife's needs? How can your words help to meet those needs and benefit them?

Sit down with your spouse, make them their favourite drink, and then build them up with some loving conversation.

'Honour one another
above yourselves.'
Romans 12:10

When we are lifting each
other up, rather than
tearing each other down,
we are both honoured.

What could you do to honour your spouse today?

Be creative and design a simple certificate, award or trophy to give to your spouse, celebrating something that you appreciate about them. Or buy a card, helium balloon or flowers in honour of their uniqueness.

'Be devoted to
one another.'

Romans 12:10

Make each other your
number one priority, after
your relationship with God.

What does being devoted
mean to you? How does the
strength of your devotion
for your spouse show in the
things you do and say?

Do something today to
show your husband or wife
how devoted you are.

'Jesus said to the servants, "Fill the jars with water"; so they filled them to the brim.'

John 2:7

Jesus took what was available at the wedding in Cana and transformed it into something amazing.

Sometimes your marriage
can feel as if it has no
more 'wine' left to offer.

But Jesus can take
whatever you have
available, even plain or
polluted water, and
transform it with his
miraculous love. He needs
your help, too, but it's
worth the effort.

'But thanks be to God, who
. . . through us spreads
everywhere the fragrance
of the knowledge of him.'
2 Corinthians 2:14

The more we know God, the
more his fragrance can
diffuse through our lives
to those around us.

How can you both grow in your knowledge of God so that his fragrance can flow through each of you into your marriage?

How can the fragrance of your God-centred marriage improve the atmosphere in the places where you live, work, worship and play?

**'Rejoice with those
who rejoice.'**
Romans 12:15

**Being happy on your own
can be a little sad.**

Make a list of at least
twenty things in your life
and home that you're
both happy about.

Choose one and celebrate
this special thing in a new
and unusual way – make a
cake, create a refreshing
drink, plant a tree!

**'Mourn with those
who mourn.'**
Romans 12:15

**Being sad on your own can
be very sad indeed.**

Discuss how each of you might like the other one to respond when you're feeling sad or discouraged.

Be specific and offer your husband or wife a few ideas to help him or her respond in the most comforting way when you're sad.

'Live in harmony with
one another.'

Romans 12:16

Living in harmony doesn't
mean we agree about
everything. Musical
harmony involves a range
of different notes that
sound good together.

What are some of the
discordant chords in your
marriage? Where do
your differences clash
together in a noisy way?

How can you find a way to
appreciate one another's
different approaches to a
challenging issue, so
that you can live together
more harmoniously?

'Accept one another,
then, just as
Christ accepted you.'

Romans 15:7

The greatest gift we can
offer someone who has
failed miserably is to
welcome him or
her as if they have
succeeded incredibly.

When does your spouse
most need your
acceptance?

Take a few minutes to
reflect on the amazing
acceptance that Jesus has
shown to you, and then
think of some ways in which
you can show that same
generous acceptance to
your husband or wife.

'I thank my God every
time I remember you.'

Philippians 1:3

The more often we thank
God for our husband or
wife, the more our love
for them will grow.

Make a list of thirty-one
things about your spouse
that you can thank God for.

Then say thank you to God,
and your spouse, for one
of these things every
day for a month. What
difference does your
'gratitude attitude' make
to your relationship?

'Each of you should look
not only to your own
interests, but also to
the interests of others.'

Philippians 2:4

Love helps the other
person to reach their
goals, because when
they succeed, we
have succeeded, too.

Draw a life-map together
of the journey you've
made as a couple so far.

Then add a road into the
future, showing the things
you'd like to achieve
personally, and as a couple,
in the next few years.

'Let your gentleness
be evident to all.'
Philippians 4:5

Sometimes our gentleness
is more evident towards
the people around us
who are strangers than
the people around us
in our family!

Who would describe you as gentle? What evidence would they have for describing you in that way?

Take the time to do something gentle for your spouse. You could massage their hands or feet with body butter, or let them relax while you do their chores.

'Whatever is true . . . noble
. . . right . . . pure . . .
lovely . . . admirable
– if anything is excellent
or praiseworthy – think
about such things.'

Philippians 4:8

It's said that we become
like the things we think
about. So our thoughts
have a very powerful effect
on our relationships.

What positive thoughts
can you choose to have
that will help you to be
the best husband or
wife you could be?

Write a letter to your
spouse describing the ways
in which he or she is true,
noble, right, pure, lovely,
admirable, excellent
and praiseworthy.

'Bear with each other
and forgive whatever
grievances you may have
against one another.
Forgive as the Lord
forgave you.'
Colossians 3:13

One of the most powerful
routes to forgiveness
is listening to the ways in
which our unloving
behaviour has hurt
the one we love.

Is there something you've done that hurt your spouse? Encourage them to tell you how they felt so that you can begin a healthy healing process together.

When your spouse asks you for forgiveness, remember how much God has forgiven you, and then find a way to pass that forgiveness on to your spouse.

'May the Lord make your love increase and overflow for each other and for everyone else.'

1 Thessalonians 3:12

When God's love flows through your life and your marriage, his love also overflows into the lives of the people in your family, community and church.

How can you be reminded
to do something every
day to help your husband
or wife feel more and
more loved the longer
you are together?

Carry out an act of
kindness as a couple that
will show God's love to
someone needing
encouragement.

'Encourage one another
and build each other up.'

1 Thessalonians 5:11

When we build each other
up, we build a stronger wall
around our marriage.

**What encouragement does
your husband or wife
need today?**

**Say or do at least one thing
today to encourage your
spouse towards one of his
or her personal goals.
See if you can think up a
creative or surprising way
to encourage them.**

'If any of you lacks wisdom,
he should ask God, who
gives generously to all
without finding fault, and
it will be given to him.'

James 1:5

When your relationship
seems complicated
and you don't know how
to mend it, God knows.
Ask him for wisdom.

When your relationship gets stuck, remember that this is normal, and every marriage faces challenges occasionally.

Pray about finding a trustworthy person, such as a pastor or counsellor, to help you through the crisis. A counsellor is much cheaper than a divorce lawyer!

'Let us not love with
words or tongue but with
actions and in truth.'
1 John 3:18

It's wonderful to hear
the words 'I love you',
but it can be even more
wonderful to experience
that love in action.

Make a list of twelve things
the other person has done
that helped you feel
especially loved.

Swap lists and discover
how your spouse likes to
be loved. Looking at their
list, what loving things
would you like to do
more of in the future?

'No one has ever seen God;
but if we love one another,
God lives in us and his love
is made complete in us.'

1 John 4:12

You are the person,
chosen by God, to be
the best channel of his
love to your spouse.

How can you help your
spouse to have a richer
experience of God's love
through your marriage?

Think about what an
ever-loving God would
most like you to do
to help your spouse
experience his love?
Then ask him to
help you do it.

'There is no fear in
love. But perfect love
drives out fear.'
1 John 4:18

Fear crushes love, and love
crushes fear. They can't
live together.

What are the greatest
fears you and your spouse
have in your marriage?

Do whatever you can to
dissolve your spouse's
fears with your perfect
love. Be gentle. Drive
slower. Lock the doors.
Spend and save carefully.
Avoid developing
friendships with those of
the opposite sex. . . .

'The only thing that
counts is faith expressing
itself through love.'
Galatians 5:6

Our faith in God becomes
real when we depend on
him to transform our
made-on-earth
marriage into something
out of this world.

How does your faith in God
inspire your love for
one another and enrich
your marriage?

Imagine the marriage God
would like you both to
enjoy, and depend on him
to provide everything
your relationship needs to
make his dream for your
marriage come true.

'Devote yourselves to
prayer, being watchful
and thankful.'
Colossians 4:2

Praying *with* each other
can be challenging, but
you can always find ways
to pray *for* each other
and *for* your marriage.
Share your prayer requests
and thank God for the
answers he sends.

Take a few moments to
pray for one another.
Tell one another your
prayer requests and
then hold hands and pray
together silently.

Squeeze your spouse's
hand when you've finished
praying, and then say
'Amen' together.

'Whoever sows generously
will also reap generously.'

2 Corinthians 9:6

The more love we invest in
our relationships, the more
love we'll receive in return.

How can you show
generosity to your spouse?
What kind of generosity do
you think he or she most
needs to experience today?

Make a list of five ways you
can be generous to your
spouse today. Then be very
generous and do all five!

'Greater love has no one
than this, that he lay down
his life for his friends.'

John 15:13

Even a small sacrifice,
inspired by love,
is precious.

What is God calling you
to sacrifice for the sake
of your marriage?
Perhaps it's your hobby
time, long work hours,
a promotion, some money,
your pride . . . ?

Give up one thing this
week to show your spouse
how much he or she
means to you.

'Blessed are those
who mourn, for they
will be comforted.'
Matthew 5:4

One of the best things
about being sad is having
someone we love to
come and comfort us.

How does your spouse
like to be comforted?
With words, a loving touch,
or a listening ear and
a box of tissues?

The next time your spouse
is sad about something, ask,
'What can I do to comfort
you?' and then do it.

'Many waters cannot quench love; rivers cannot wash it away.'

Song of Songs 8:7

Nothing can destroy the powerful bond of love.

What are some of the challenges your marriage has overcome?

Make a list of the challenges that you have faced as a couple and make another list of the ways in which each challenge has strengthened your marriage. Then celebrate some of your victories together!

'Enjoy life with your
wife, whom you love.'
Ecclesiastes 9:9

Joy is being married to
your best friend!

What are some of the
things you enjoyed doing
as a couple when you
first met?

Have a date doing some
of the things you did
before you were married.
Ride bikes, have a picnic,
hire a boat, talk late
into the night. . . .

'There is a time for
everything . . .
a time to embrace.'

Ecclesiastes 3:1, 5

Hugging can dissolve
stress, soothe tension
and help us feel closer
to one another.

When do you most like to
be hugged? When does
your spouse most like
to be hugged? What have
you learned about hugging
from thinking about
these two questions?

Find a quiet time to share a
hug and enjoy just being
close together.

'A cheerful heart is
good medicine.'
Proverbs 17:22

**Happiness heals hearts
as well as bodies.**

What do you and your spouse enjoy laughing at together? How can you add more humour to your lives?

Reminisce about the funny things that have happened to you as a couple. Maybe you could collect the stories in a notebook.

'By wisdom a house is built,
and through understanding
it is established; through
knowledge its rooms are
filled with rare and
beautiful treasures.'

Proverbs 24:3, 4

The more we understand
one another, the more
secure our relationship
can become.

Take the time to ask some gentle questions so that you can understand one another better.

Use what you know about your spouse to help you plan a rare and beautiful moment that will create a memory for you both to treasure together.

'He who finds a wife finds
what is good and receives
favour from the Lord.'

Proverbs 18:22

**God delights in your
marriage!**

List some of the blessings
that God has added to your
life because you're married
to your husband or wife.

Thank your loved one for
being a channel through
which God blesses your life.

'A friend loves at all times.'
Proverbs 17:17

A spouse loves at all
times, too, even though
the temperature gauge
may fluctuate from
time to time.

When do you feel most in love with your husband or wife? How can you experience that love more often?

To keep your love burning strong: plan to do something loving for your spouse every day, however you feel. It's a marriage-saving experiment worth trying.

'A gentle answer turns away wrath, but a harsh word stirs up anger.'

Proverbs 15:1

When we choose how we respond, we help to choose how our spouse will respond.

Look out for patterns in your relationship and notice when one of you is more likely to become angry or irritated.

Find a gentle way to respond to your husband or wife that will defuse his or her anger or frustration, and not add to the irritation.

'But the fruit of the Spirit
is love, joy, peace,
patience, kindness,
goodness, faithfulness,
gentleness and self-control.'
Galatians 5:22, 23

Inviting the Holy Spirit
into your lives can make a
life-changing difference
to the atmosphere in
your marriage.

Draw nine lines on a piece of paper and make a scale from 0-10 along each line. Indicate how much of each Spirit-fruit you think you are producing.

What can you do to show more of each Spirit-fruit quality in your marriage?

'I belong to my lover,
and his desire is for me.'
Song of Songs 7:10

When we know we're
desired we become
more desirable.

Tell your spouse how
desirable you find
him or her.

If you find it hard to talk,
write your thoughts in
a letter, or express
your desire through
loving touch.

'He has made everything
beautiful in its time.'
Ecclesiastes 3:11

Beautiful things can take
years to create. It took
thirty-three years to
complete the ceiling of
the Sistine Chapel.
Michelangelo was often in
great discomfort as he lay
on the wooden boards just
below his paintings.

What aspects of your
marriage is God beautifying
right now? How can you
work with him on this
valuable project?

Find an object together
that illustrates something
beautiful about your
marriage and place it in
your home where you'll
see it every day.

'If two lie down together,
they will keep warm.
But how can one keep
warm alone?'

Ecclesiastes 4:11

So many things in life are
easier and better when
there are two of you.

Are there some things that either of you struggles with doing alone? How can you support one another?

Choose a task that neither of you likes doing, and then do it together, finding ways to make it as fun and enjoyable as possible!

'Practise hospitality.'
Romans12:13

**Sometimes the person who
needs our hospitality the
most is the person we
live with every day.**

How different would your marriage be if you treated one another like guests?

What positive effect would this have on the way you speak to one another, and the ways in which you serve one another?

'Submit to one another out
of reverence for Christ.'
Ephesians 5:21

**A successful marriage
needs two people who
are willing and able to
submit to one another.**

When did you last submit
to the wishes of your
husband or wife?
What effect did it have
on your marriage?

Look for a way, however
small, to submit to
the wishes of your
spouse today.

'Wives, submit to your
husbands as to the Lord.'
Ephesians 5:22

The most important person
to submit to, as a husband
or wife, is God himself.

What difference does it make to your marriage when you submit to God first? Are there areas in your marriage where you have been rebelling against God's will?

Listen to what God is asking you to do to help you build an even closer relationship with him and with one another.

'Husbands, love your wives,
just as Christ loved
the church and gave
himself up for her.'

Ephesians 5:25

God challenges us to love
our husband or wife as
much as Jesus loved us
and died for us!

Spend time reading about
the last days of Jesus'
life and understanding
how much he loves you
(John chapters 13-20).

Let his love for you fill up
your heart so that you have
more of his love to share
with your husband or wife.

' "Love the Lord your God with all your heart and with all your soul and with all your mind." This is the first and greatest commandment. And the second is like it: "Love your neighbour as yourself." '

Matthew 22:37-39

Love God, and then love your husband or wife as much as you love yourself.

How can you love your spouse with all your heart and soul and mind? And how can you express this amazing love to your husband or wife?

How can you and your spouse find a way to share God's love with your neighbours?

'Therefore what God has joined together, let man not separate.'

Matthew 19:6

God has given you to one another, as a gift, and he wants to do all he can to keep your marriage growing and happy.

What is the greatest
threat to your marriage
and how can you invite
God to protect your
relationship?

Work with God today by
doing something that will
bring you closer together
as a couple. Talk together,
discuss a Bible passage,
play together and pray
together.

'A cord of three strands
is not quickly broken.'
Ecclesiastes 4:12

The cord of marriage is
stronger when God is
the first strand, and
you are both bound
together with him.

What place does your faith have in your marriage? Is God the strong cord in your marriage, or have you let his strand fray?

Take at least five minutes a day to read the Bible together and discuss what it means to each of you.

' "For I know the plans I have for you," declares the Lord, "plans to prosper you and not to harm you, plans to give you hope and a future." '

Jeremiah 29:11

God has great plans for your marriage!

What plans do you think
God has for your marriage?
What plans do each of you
have for your marriage?

How do these future plans
fit together, or do you
need to adjust some of
your own ideas?

'And now these three
remain: faith, hope and
love. But the greatest
of these is love.'

1 Corinthians 13:13

Love is the most powerful
gift that God has ever
given us. It needs to be
expressed or it will die.

How do faith, hope and love
work together to encourage
you in your marriage?

Make a collection of
objects, pictures and
stories that have
helped you to understand
what loving your
spouse really means.
Show them to one another.

If God were to bless your
marriage, what do you
think he would say?

Take a few moments to
write a short blessing
for your husband or wife,
and then speak the
words over one another
as you hold hands.

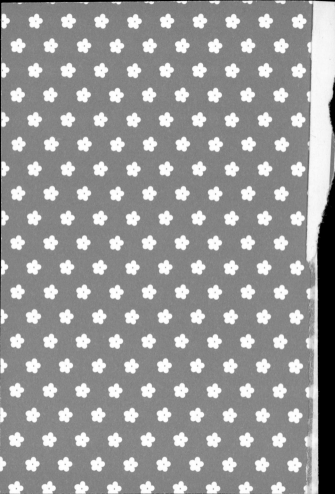

OWL
WISDOM

Zoe Bell

summersdale

OWL WISDOM

Summersdale Publishers Ltd
46 West Street
Chichester
West Sussex
PO19 1RP
UK

www.summersdale.com

Printed and bound in the Czech Republic

ISBN: 978-1-84953-722-3

Substantial discounts on bulk quantities of Summersdale
books are available to corporations, professional associations
and other organisations. For details contact Nicky Douglas by
telephone: +44 (0) 1243 756902, fax: +44 (0) 1243 786300
or email: nicky@summersdale.com.

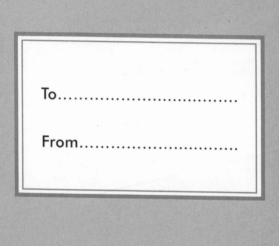

To....................................

From................................

Whatever you can do or
dream you can, begin
it. Boldness has genius,
power and magic in it.

JOHANN WOLFGANG VON GOETHE

Let your hook
always be cast; in
the pool where you
least expect
it, there will be fish.

OVID

Love yourself first
and everything else
falls into line.

LUCILLE BALL

I can't change the
direction of the wind,
but I can adjust my sails
to always reach
my destination.

JAMES DEAN

Opportunities are like sunrises. If you wait too long, you miss them.

WILLIAM ARTHUR WARD

If you're going to be thinking anything, you might as well think big.

DONALD TRUMP

If we had no winter,
the spring would not
be so pleasant.

ANNE BRADSTREET

He has achieved
success who has lived
well, laughed often,
and loved much.

BESSIE ANDERSON STANLEY

All life is an experiment.
The more experiments
you make the better.

RALPH WALDO EMERSON

You only get one
chance at life and you
have to grab it boldly.

BEAR GRYLLS

*Be faithful to
that which exists
nowhere but in
yourself.*

ANDRÉ GIDE

Don't save things for a special occasion. Every day of your life is a special occasion.

THOMAS S. MONSON

Things do not happen. Things are made to happen.

JOHN F. KENNEDY

Life is a great **big canvas;** throw all the **paint** you can at it.

DANNY KAYE

There is nothing
impossible to him
who will try.

ALEXANDER THE GREAT

Follow your own star!

DANTE ALIGHIERI

Wherever you go,
no matter what the
weather, always bring
your own sunshine.

ANTHONY J. D'ANGELO

Set your goals high, and don't stop till you get there.

BO JACKSON

It's all right to have **butterflies** in your stomach. Just get them to **fly in formation**.

ROB GILBERT

Opportunity does
not knock, it presents
itself when you beat
down the door.

KYLE CHANDLER

*Enthusiasm
moves the world.*

ARTHUR BALFOUR

You can, you should,
and if you're brave
enough to start, you will.

STEPHEN KING

When you're true to
who you are, amazing
things happen.

DEBORAH NORVILLE

The man who
removes a
mountain
begins by
carrying
away small
stones.

CHINESE PROVERB

I have found that if
you love life, life will
love you back.

ARTHUR RUBINSTEIN

For myself I am an
optimist – it does not
seem to be much use
being anything else.

WINSTON CHURCHILL

Mix a little foolishness
with your serious plans.
It is lovely to be silly at
the right moment.

HORACE

Where there is great love there are always miracles.

WILLA CATHER

One way to get the
most out of life
is to look upon it as an
adventure.

WILLIAM FEATHER

Do not wait: the time will never be 'just right'.

NAPOLEON HILL

Life shrinks or expands in proportion to one's courage.

ANAÏS NIN

If you think you are too small to make a difference, try sleeping with a mosquito.

DALAI LAMA

If you don't like how
things are, change it!
You're not a tree.

JIM ROHN

It is in your moments
of decision that your
destiny is shaped.

TONY ROBBINS

To fight fear, act. To increase fear – wait, put off, postpone.

DAVID JOSEPH SCHWARTZ

Aerodynamically the bumble bee shouldn't be able to fly, but the bumblebee doesn't know it so it goes on flying anyway.

MARY KAY ASH

Tell me, what is it you plan
to do with your one wild
and precious life?

MARY OLIVER

Life is a helluva lot more fun if you say yes rather than no.

RICHARD BRANSON

The **best** **way** to predict your future is to **create it.**

ABRAHAM LINCOLN

Our **best successes** often come after our greatest disappointments.

HENRY WARD BEECHER

Always laugh when you can. It is cheap medicine.

LORD BYRON

Don't judge each
day by the harvest
you reap but by the
seeds that you plant.

ROBERT LOUIS STEVENSON

*Everything in
our life should be
based on love.*

RAY BRADBURY

In dreams and in
love there are no
impossibilities.

JÁNOS ARANY

No great thing is
created suddenly.

EPICTETUS

Setting goals is the
first step in turning the
invisible into the visible.

TONY ROBBINS

A happy life consists not in the absence, but in the mastery of hardships.

HELEN KELLER

Opportunity dances with those already on the dance floor.

H. JACKSON BROWN JR

The thing to do is
enjoy the ride while
you're on it.

JOHNNY DEPP

Mistakes are the
portals of discovery.

JAMES JOYCE

What we need is more people who specialise in the impossible.

THEODORE ROETHKE

*If you learn
from defeat, you
haven't really lost.*

ZIG ZIGLAR

Angels can fly because they take themselves **lightly**.

G. K. CHESTERTON

It takes courage to grow up and become who you really are.

E. E. CUMMINGS

Shoot for the moon. Even if you miss, you'll land among the stars.

LES BROWN

Throw caution to the
wind and just do it.

CARRIE UNDERWOOD

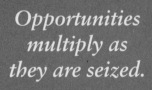

*Opportunities
multiply as
they are seized.*

SUN TZU

You're the blacksmith of
your own happiness.

SWEDISH PROVERB

Every day holds the
possibility of a miracle.

ELIZABETH DAVID

Keep smiling, because life is a beautiful thing and there's so much to smile about.

MARILYN MONROE

One may walk over the
highest mountain one
step at a time.

JOHN WANAMAKER

Until you're ready to look foolish, you'll never have the possibility of being great.

CHER

A life spent making mistakes is not only more honourable, but more useful than a life spent doing nothing.

GEORGE BERNARD SHAW

Time goes on. So
whatever you're
going to do, do it. Do
it now. Don't wait.

ROBERT DE NIRO

Find something you're
passionate about and
keep tremendously
interested in it.

JULIA CHILD

Life will always be to a large extent what we ourselves make it.

SAMUEL SMILES

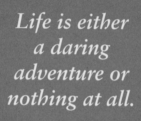

Life is either a daring adventure or nothing at all.

HELEN KELLER

Plunge boldly into the thick of life, and seize it where you will, it is always interesting.

JOHANN WOLFGANG VON GOETHE

The purpose of life is to live it, to taste experience to the utmost, to reach out eagerly and without fear for newer and richer experience.

ELEANOR ROOSEVELT

Be yourself.
The world worships the original.

INGRID BERGMAN

We do not remember
days, we remember
moments.

CESARE PAVESE

If you love life, don't waste time, for time is what life is made up of.

BRUCE LEE

There are no traffic jams
along the extra mile.

ROGER STAUBACH

In order to succeed, we must first believe that we can.

NIKOS KAZANTZAKIS

What we see depends mainly on what we look for.

JOHN LUBBOCK

*Give out what
you most want to
see come back.*

ROBIN SHARMA

Put your heart, mind, and soul into even your smallest acts. This is the secret of success.

SIVĀNANDA SARASWATI

He is a wise man who
does not grieve for the
things which he has not,
but rejoices for those
which he has.

EPICTETUS

*My best friend is
the one who brings
out the best in me.*

HENRY FORD

Change your thoughts
and you change
your world.

NORMAN VINCENT PEALE

Feelings are much like waves, we can't stop them from coming but we can choose which one to surf.

JONATHAN MÅRTENSSON

Do your little
bit of **good**
where you are;
it's those little
bits of good put
together
that overwhelm
the world.

DESMOND TUTU

You can't use up
creativity. The more you
use, the more you have.

MAYA ANGELOU

Every day is an
opportunity to make a
new happy ending.

ANONYMOUS

Life is really simple, but
we insist on making it
complicated.

CONFUCIUS

The most important kind
of freedom is to be what
you really are.

JIM MORRISON

There was never a night
or a problem that could
defeat sunrise or hope.

BERNARD WILLIAMS

Always be a first-rate
version of yourself,
instead of a second-rate
version of somebody else.

JUDY GARLAND

Dream as if you'll live forever. Live as if you'll die today.

JAMES DEAN

Your present
circumstances
don't determine
where you can
go; they merely
**determine
where you
start.**

NIDO QUBEIN

Only those who will
risk going too far can
possibly find out how
far one can go.

T. S. ELIOT

Understand that the right to choose your own path is a sacred privilege. Use it. Dwell in possibility.

OPRAH WINFREY

Be eccentric now.
Don't wait for old age
to wear purple.

REGINA BRETT

The best and most
beautiful things in the
world cannot be seen
or even touched – they
must be felt with the
heart.

HELEN KELLER

The secret of happiness
is the determination
to be happy always,
rather than wait for outer
circumstances to make
one happy.

J. DONALD WALTERS

Cherish your visions and your dreams as they are the children of your soul; the blueprints of your ultimate achievements.

NAPOLEON HILL

When you have a dream,
you've got to grab it
and never let go.

CAROL BURNETT

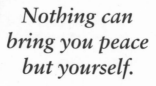

Nothing can bring you peace but yourself.

RALPH WALDO EMERSON

If we all did the things we are **capable** of, we would literally **astound** ourselves.

THOMAS EDISON

Let your hopes, not your hurts, shape your future.

ROBERT H. SCHULLER

Hope is a talent
like any other.

STORM JAMESON

A friend is someone who
gives you total freedom
to be yourself.

JIM MORRISON

Your time is limited, so don't waste it living someone else's life.

STEVE JOBS

You ask me what I
came into this life to
do, I will tell you: I came
to live out loud.

ÉMILE ZOLA

When you dance to your own rhythm, life taps its toes to your beat.

TERRI GUILLEMETS

Every moment is
a fresh beginning.

T. S. ELIOT

Very little is needed to make a happy life; it is all within yourself, in your way of thinking.

MARCUS AURELIUS

If you do not **change direction**, you may end up where you are heading.

LAO TZU

He who trims himself to suit everyone will soon whittle himself away.

RAYMOND HULL

Let your soul stand cool
and composed before a
million universes.

WALT WHITMAN

Life is not measured by
the number of breaths
you take, but by the
moments that take your
breath away.

ANONYMOUS

First say to yourself what you would be; and then do what you have to do.

EPICTETUS

We will always tend to
fulfil our own expectation
of ourselves.

BRIAN TRACY

Look at life through the windshield, not the rear-view mirror.

BYRD BAGGETT

You are always
free to change
your mind
and choose a
different future, or
a different past.

RICHARD BACH

Life begins at the end of
your comfort zone.

NEALE DONALD WALSCH

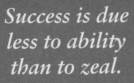

Success is due less to ability than to zeal.

CHARLES BUXTON

To be yourself in a world
that is constantly trying
to make you something
else is the greatest
accomplishment.

RALPH WALDO EMERSON

The purpose of life
is to be happy.

DALAI LAMA

We must
accept finite
disappointment,
but never
lose infinite
hope.

MARTIN LUTHER KING JR

Life is short. Kiss slowly,
laugh insanely, love truly
and forgive quickly.

PAULO COELHO

In a gentle way, you can shake the world.

MAHATMA GANDHI

If you have good thoughts they will shine out of your face like sunbeams and you will always look lovely.

ROALD DAHL

Believe you can and
you're halfway there.

THEODORE ROOSEVELT

Smooth seas do not
make skilful sailors.

AFRICAN PROVERB

We have more
possibilities available
in each moment
than we realise.

THÍCH NHÁT HẠNH

Change brings opportunity.

NIDO QUBEIN

They always say time changes things, but you actually have to change them yourself.

ANDY WARHOL

Don't be afraid to go
out on a limb. That's
where the fruit is.

ANONYMOUS

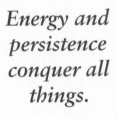

Energy and persistence conquer all things.

BENJAMIN FRANKLIN

Believe with all of your heart that you **will do** what you were made to do.

ORISON SWETT MARDEN

Self-confidence is the
first requisite to great
undertakings.

SAMUEL JOHNSON

Good friends are like
stars... you don't always
see them but you know
they're always there.

ANONYMOUS

The greatest sweetener of human life is Friendship.

JOSEPH ADDISON

Those who bring sunshine
into the lives of others
cannot keep it from
themselves.

J. M. BARRIE

The most important
thing is to enjoy your
life – to be happy –
it's all that matters.

AUDREY HEPBURN

Life is ten per cent what happens to you and ninety per cent how you respond to it.

LOU HOLTZ

Sometimes it's the smallest decisions that can change your life forever.

KERI RUSSELL

Most of us spend our lives as if we had another one in the bank.

BEN IRWIN

What great thing would you attempt if you knew you could not fail?

ROBERT H. SCHULLER

To change one's life:

1. Start immediately.
2. Do it flamboyantly.
3. No exceptions.

WILLIAM JAMES

If you don't
like something,
change it; if
you can't change
it, change the
way you think
about it.

MARY ENGELBREIT

Think big thoughts but
relish small pleasures.

H. JACKSON BROWN JR

If you change the
way you look at
things, the things you
look at change.

WAYNE DYER

Turn your face toward the
sun and the shadows will
fall behind you.

MAORI PROVERB

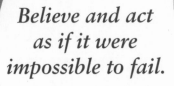

*Believe and act
as if it were
impossible to fail.*

CHARLES F. KETTERING

Be happy for this moment. This moment is your life.

OMAR KHAYYÁM

A journey of a thousand miles begins with a single step.

LAO TZU

A **friend** is one who knows you and **loves** you just the same.

ELBERT HUBBARD

Go as far as you can
see; when you get
there, you'll be able
to see further.

THOMAS CARLYLE

When life looks like it's falling apart, it may just be falling in place.

BEVERLY SOLOMON

Make each day
your masterpiece.

JOHN WOODEN

Become a possibilitarian.
No matter how dark
things seem to be or
actually are, raise your
sights and see possibilities.

NORMAN VINCENT PEALE

If opportunity doesn't
knock, build a door.

MILTON BERLE

*A loving heart
is the truest
wisdom.*

CHARLES DICKENS

The future depends
on what we do in
the present.

MAHATMA GANDHI

If you're interested in finding out more about our books, find us on Facebook at **Summersdale Publishers** and follow us on Twitter at **@Summersdale**.

www.summersdale.com